To Dani:

Life

adven

trekking.

Kathy Wall

NOT BY CHANCE

Kathy Wall

Written by: Kathy Wall

ISBN 9781735799810

Table of Contents

A New Direction

My life changed one hot Wednesday night in August.

When my youngest child was two-and-a-half, my oldest had attended a nearby church's Wednesday night kid's club with a neighbor. She had a great time and wanted to go again. My youngest was upset they wouldn't let him go too. The church didn't have a program for kiddos as young as he was.

Stubborn as I was, I decided to find a church where I could take both children. We had not attended a church in Texas since we moved here two years earlier, so the hunt was on. To my surprise, most of the churches in our area didn't hold Wednesday services in August. An acquaintance I met at the swimming pool said her church was open.

I committed to attending the service, but I

became hesitant as evening approached. Doubts flooded my thinking. I knew nothing about this girl's denomination. Did they believe what I believed? Did they have some weird practices? Were they a cult?

I decided to keep the kids with me.

I also didn't want anyone to know who I was, just in case I didn't want to come back. The woman I knew was on vacation, so I didn't expect to see anyone I knew. When I entered the church only minutes before service was to begin, I avoided the women chatting in clusters around the spacious foyer and shooed my children down the hall toward the sanctuary. I found seats as far from the foyer as I could get. The inquisitive stares of other attendees riveted me to my seat. No one bothered me, and I felt safe.

The service was pretty typical until a member of the congregation was invited to pray. When someone was asked to pray in my home church, they arrived at the pulpit with a sheet of paper to read. This man simply walked up to the stage, picked up a remote microphone, and started praying. I had never seen such a thing.

Goosebumps covered my arms. Why had I brought my children here?

These people were different. I hugged my kids a little closer. There was nothing wrong about what he said, but this place was definitely unusual. My defense ramparts rose.

Following a short sermon, the pastor called for testimonies.

What? Testimonies? My pulse rate and panic soared.

A long silence made everyone squirm except me. I was ready to leave. Then one little lady stood up. As she spoke, I became increasingly uncomfortable.

Who were these people? What did they actually believe? What other unusual rituals did they practice?

When the second person stood, I located the exits and planned a sudden departure. I prepared so when I heard the final amen, I would rush my kids out the exit as far from the foyer as possible. We would hurry to the car around the outside of the building. With any luck, we could avoid contact with anyone.

An undercurrent of amens and hallelujahs followed each testimony.

After seven or eight people testified, I was a nervous wreck. This testimony thing was really bizarre.

Would these people jump up and dance down the aisles?

I reviewed my escape plan. Fear continued to rise. If anyone had touched me at that moment, I would have screamed.

A long silence signaled the end of the service. My heart rate slowed, and I began to relax. Surely the benediction would be soon.

As I bent to whisper about leaving to my children, an older man directly behind me stood.

"I just wanted to tell you what happened to me today."

Both my kids turned to look at him. I didn't. But

everyone else in the congregation did. Were they looking at him, or me? My nerves tingled.

"We were teasing a guy at work because he was late. The man said that while he drove to the office, the woman in front of him ran a stop sign in a school zone and…and…"

He gripped the pew so hard his fingers turned white. One hand was inches from my shoulder. I stared at his gnarled fingers. My kids stared at him.

The amen chorus resumed cloaking the silence with an undercurrent of murmurings.

He continued. "And she hit a kid and he died. Right there."

Gasps rang out around the room.

The man rocked forward. Tears splattered on the back of the pew.

Wow, this man was really worked up over a total stranger's accident.

"I just wanted to praise God." He choked up and openly sobbed.

My kids froze on the pew. They had never seen a

man weep.

How could he praise God for a child dying? And to cry in public! My heart rate skyrocketed, and I could barely breathe. Prepared to run, I signaled the kids to scoot closer.

“I want to praise God, because when I was nine, a lady ran a stop sign in a school zone and hit me. It’s by God’s grace I’m here today. I want to thank Him for what He did. Not only for saving my life but for letting me be a member of His family.”

The chorus erupted in a single resounding hallelujah followed by mutterings of agreement, understanding, and approval.

My heart stilled. My resistance crumbled. This man—these people—knew God in a way I didn’t even know was possible. I suddenly wanted to know Him for more than a deity to worship on Sunday mornings. My innermost being growled with a hunger for a personal relationship like these people demonstrated.

“Lord,” I whispered, “help me to know You.”

That instant, my walk *with* God began. It's been an amazing journey.

* * *

The following stories represent some of the events along my trek with God since that Wednesday night in Texas. The conversations aren't exact quotes but are representative of the events. Names were deliberately eliminated except to highlight settings. The narratives are not in chronological order.

If you don't know Christ as your Savior, these stories won't make much sense. To you, they will read like fiction (none are), or you'll chalk it up to circumstances. If you react like that, stop reading and seek Jesus. He's inviting you to join His family or to a closer relationship.

Those who do have a relationship with Christ will understand and will sometimes say "Amen" or "Hallelujah." Even an occasional "Wow" or "Praise the Lord."

These stories are by no means promises from God, or even a pattern of His behavior, but they do show the character of God. They are simply how God dealt with me.

My desire is that you find encouragement and inspiration to grow in your relationship with God. Your walk will be unique, and, one day, you will have stories to share.

My Mistake

Not long after I learned the difference between being a believer and being a follower of Jesus Christ, I visited my mother in Atlanta for Thanksgiving. True to her nature, my mom and two of her dear friends decided they would go to the mall on Black Friday. This was years ago when Black Friday was a big event that didn't start until 10 am on Friday.

I don't enjoy shopping, and I detest crowds. Not a good combination for an outing on the biggest shopping day of the year at the busiest mall in Georgia. I barely knew my mother's friends, but they weren't on my list of favorite people. I decided to stay home and watch football games.

But my mother insisted it would be a bonding experience and pressed the issue until I relented. Within minutes, a car with her friends turned into our driveway.

I renamed my mom's friends Bossy and Sweetie. The secret names were perfect for their personalities.

Bossy drove. My mother and I got into the back seat.

Traffic crawled around the mall.

"Where do you think we should park?" Bossy asked.

I glanced out the window at the lines of cars entering the parking lot. "Where do you want to shop?"

"At Nordstrom's. Where else?" Bossy snapped.

"Then go there." It seemed such a logical response.

"But," Bossy challenged, "everyone loves that store and their lot will be full."

Before I thought, I opened my mouth. "If you need a parking place there, we'll just ask God to get us one."

I saw the hairs rise on Bossy's neck. "So, you think your God will find us a parking place on Black

Friday?"

"Of course." I still wasn't thinking.

She sped up on the access road and headed for Nordstrom's lot. "Then you'd better get to asking."

My mother fisted her hands and crossed her arms over her chest, showing her total disapproval of what I had said.

As we approached from the ramp, we could scan the whole lot. The one-way drive snaked around ten or twelve rows to the store entrance then made a straight shot to the exit. Once you entered the drive, you had to go the entire route to get out.

A red car was two rows ahead of us as Bossy turned into the lot.

"I don't see any open spaces." Sarcasm dripped from her words. "But since Kathy's been talking to her God, we'll give it a shot anyway."

What had I done? I made a statement that God would do something without even asking Him. I had put God in the position of being mocked and ridiculed. It was wrong. Oh, so wrong.

Oh Lord. I'm sorry. I should never have said such a thing. What do I do now?

Bossy followed the serpentine drive. I'm sure she drove slower than she ever had in her life just to make a point.

Halfway across the parking lot, our driver stretched her head forward and turned slowly from side to side as she looked for a spot. "Not a space in sight."

Sweetie glanced into the back seat. "Perhaps someone will leave by the time we get there."

"Ha!" Bossy snarled. "I have eyes, I can see. No one has left the store since we started down this goose chase. You can see there are no open slots in this section. Guess you got it wrong, Kathy." She cackled.

My entire body burned. I had flippantly put the name of the God of the universe on the line. *Lord, what should I say?* I could think of no response.

As we turned down each row, Bossy announced there were no places available.

Otherwise, silence thundered in the car.

We turned the corner on the next to last row.

"No one is leaving," the driver harassed. "I see nothing open." She almost sang. "Only one short row to go! The red car has already given up."

I searched the last two rows, hoping to see an opening. Car roofs stretched from one end to the other.

Our car slowed as we rounded the last corner and started down the row. Bossy slammed the brakes to the floor, almost throwing Sweetie into the dash. Right there, beside the entrance to the store, was an empty parking place. The prime slot in the entire area. She stared at the space for a full thirty seconds before she pulled in.

No one spoke, especially not me.

I saw God's mercy that morning. He was gracious to me. I made a mistake, and he saved me from tarnishing His reputation.

I learned my lesson. I have the right to ask, but I do not have the right to tell the God of Creation what

He should do. He did not die on the cross to grant me favors.

That was also the last time I went shopping on Black Friday.

I Believe in Miracles

Half a lifetime ago, I had gallbladder surgery. At that time, I spent three days in the hospital awaiting the procedure because required tests must be completed to prevent malpractice suits. Everyone knew I needed the surgery, but rules are rules. Friday morning, I was wheeled into OR.

The two-hour operation took three times as long as expected. When the surgeon removed the diseased organ, it ruptured, spewing infection throughout my abdominal cavity. The extra time was necessary to clean out as much infection as possible.

My fever shot up to 103.8. I was put on every available antibiotic. None worked.

Three days later, my husband was told potential outcomes. Number one on the list was death, followed closely by long-term coma. Almost as an afterthought, the doctors added brain damage ranging from barely functional to semi-normal as a third scenario.

My husband called the church to prayer.

I was in a coma. Occasionally I'd wake up for a minute then drift back off. Once when I awoke, I felt someone sit on the end of the bed. When I opened my eyes to see who was there, the space was empty. The nurse said I smiled and said, "Jesus is here."

On day five, my fever rose to 104. I was checked every two hours for temperature, blood pressure, and pulse rate. At one-thirty in the morning, my temp was 104.2. Blood pressure 65/40, ten points lower than an hour earlier. Pulse rate 155 and rising. I was not expected to survive the night.

In the weeks prior to going to the hospital, I directed part of the children's choir in a presentation on Nebuchadnezzar. When the king said, "Your God is the King of kings," My little choir shouted, "Our God is the King of kings."

The king continued, "Your God is the Lord of

lords." My kids shouted, "Our God is the Lord of lords."

Then, "Your God is the God of gods." The kids yelled at the top of their lungs, "Our God is the God of gods."

The next line was, "Our God is the God of gods. He rules over everything on earth."

At two a.m. in the sterile, silent hospital, I sat up in my bed and yelled (as I had taught the kids to do), "My God is the King of kings. My God is the Lord of lords, My God is the God of gods."

By the time I completed the chorus, I had two doctors and three nurses in the room.

I smiled at them and repeated the next line of the song. "My God rules over everything on earth."

I rested against the raised mattress while they checked my vitals—three times. All three readings were the same. Temperature 98.6, blood pressure120/80, pulse 75.

I inquired what day it was and about the weather.

One of the nurses called the primary surgeon on

the bedside phone. She relayed the message then said, “Yes, sir…yes, sir…yes, sir.” Then hung up.

As she walked around the end of the bed, another nurse asked what the doctor said. They both looked at me as she answered. “He said, we’ve witnessed a miracle.”

I burrowed against my pillow and whispered, “Thank you, Jesus.”

Three days later, I walked out of the hospital.

I believe in miracles because I am one.

A Big Bundle

Last October while visiting the craft group at church, I learned they needed beanies to give to the men at the homeless shelter for Christmas. A lot of beanies. I was given a pattern and went home to begin making the hats.

I told the Lord I'd make beanies as long as I had yarn in the house. I had several skeins left over from other projects, so I thought I could make five or six hats. My contribution to a worthy cause would also clean out my closet.

With this objective in mind, I searched for skeins of yarn in the nooks where I stored leftover supplies. I found lots. Tan bundles in the sewing room, green and blue ones in the closet, and red in a box of sewing supplies. Time to get to work.

After the third beanie, the crocheting became fun.

I also began to vary the pattern. The solid hats were nice, but a stripe or two made them pop. Those tiny balls of yarn that I thought were good for nothing became the accents on these caps. So cute.

By the time I finished the second skein of tan, I had no colors in my stash to make the stripe. I needed one contrasting color. I could reverse the colors when I didn't have enough tan for another beanie and use up every scrap of both skeins. I would invest $10 or $12 in the project.

I stopped by Michael's on the way to Bible study to find the perfect accent color. You'd think something as simple as finding one skein of coordinating yarn would be easy. Rows and rows of beautiful colors attracted my attention, but the right one seemed to be hiding.

The sales rack! If I could find the color there, I'd be way ahead.

That's when I saw it. The largest bundle of yarn I'd ever seen. It was about eighteen inches long and at least twelve inches high. A quick estimate told me this mass of milk chocolate thread would cost as much as four or five large skeins. Way out of my budget. Besides, I didn't need any more yarn in the house.

But, how much would this five-pound chunk of yarn actually cost? My curiosity got the best of me, and I asked a salesclerk to check it out.

While she was away, I decided if the bundle cost less than $20, I'd buy it. At that price, it'd be a bargain.

While waiting, I found a brown and orange variegated yarn for the stripes on my crème hats.

The salesclerk returned and handed me the bundle. "Sorry that took so long. This yarn is discontinued and discounted so it's only in the main computer. It costs $7.99."

I hugged the huge skein and headed for checkout. That bundle would keep me busy a while. And the accent for the tan hats was a perfect match for this chocolate color too.

Beanies for the homeless. Guess I was going to

make more that I planned.

A week later, my husband went to the attic to find our fall decorations. He returned without the pumpkins but carried a box of yarn. Inside were a dozen or more full skeins. Balls of smaller amounts would provide the stripes. More beanies.

For my birthday, I received, you guessed it, more yarn. More beanies. Friends gave me their extra yarns, too.

I told the Lord I would use up the yarn in my house. My current supply came out of the woodwork (a name for attic, closet, storage room, and gifting.) I’ve made lots of hats. Even so, today I have probably ten times as much yarn as I did when I made the promise.

I’ll be busy making beanies for a while.

Bicycle Accident

Twenty years ago, when we lived in central Ohio, my husband and I rode bicycles. Not just around the block but in rides (twenty-five plus miles) and rallies (a hundred miles.) Anyone with common sense knows you don't just hop on a bike one day and ride in a rally. You train. In our case, we had prepared all summer and recently totaled two thousand miles. We were weeks away from the end of the season rally.

Saturday morning, we headed out for a seventy-five-mile ride the week before the fall rally. Our friend, who was a racer, joined us. The objective was to bike the twenty miles to a neighboring town for cinnamon rolls at a local bakery. Then our friend would return home, and we'd finish off an additional fifty-five-mile loop.

The day was beautiful. Sunny with a slight

breeze. After five miles, I noticed the racer kept pulling ahead, then slowing for us to catch up. I suggested to my husband he ride with our friend and wait for me at the stop signs. We had ridden this section many times, and I knew there was a sign about every five miles.

My husband would get a challenging workout. Our friend would enjoy the ride more. And I could take my time and not push too hard.

When I reached the snake hills, my nickname for a series of three sharp peaks, the guys were a hundred yards ahead of me. Not far past this point was the first stop sign. They zoomed down the hills and were moving pretty fast at the top of each summit.

Now it was my turn.

An odometer on the handlebars registered my speed.

Going down the first hill, I reached sixty mph. It's scary going so fast, but you have to build up speed to reach the next summit. This patch of terrain taught me when to change gears to keep moving. At the top of the second hilltop, I was going 10.4 mph. That was really good for me, as I'm usually barely moving when I reach the crest of the hills. The strength-training rides were working. One dip to go. The crest of that hill turns from a steep grade to a gradual incline.

When I reached the slope, I glanced down to be sure my feet were over the pedals. You lose a fourth of your power if your foot does not line up straight under your knee, and I tend to let my feet drift. But this time, my feet were in the correct position. No wonder I was doing so well at the crests.

As I glanced up, I noticed I was doing 13.5 mph. A new record. Then I noticed the rear wheel of our friend's bike. He was barely moving, and I was gaining rapidly. I was going to hit him!

If I swerved, I'd clip his wheel. And I was going thirteen and a half miles an hour! I braked and yelled. Later my husband reported the only thing I said was, "Go!"

It's amazing how rapidly our brains work in these

situations. If I turned, I'd probably cause him to flip sideways. If I went straight, I'd bump him, but not throw him off. Perhaps he could manage to maintain control.

Like a spacecraft docking, I lined up perfectly with the axle of his wheel. That way my leg would not come in contact with his spinning tire.

At impact, my front wheel stopped, and I went flying.

My only thought was that I hoped I wouldn't hit the handlebars with my knees. A friend had done that in an accident the year before and broke her knee cap.

The next thing I knew I was on the ground, face down. My left arm was under me, my shoulder hurt, and I could barely breathe. I was afraid I'd punctured a lung.

I tried to push up, but my arm didn't move. Broken.

My husband rushed to my side. "Are you okay?"

"No, I broke my arm." I rolled onto my back.

Breathing was easier, and it didn't hurt to suck in

air. My lungs were uninjured. I was only winded from the hard ride up that last hill. What a relief.

He reached down and picked up my hand. My arm didn't go with it. He placed it back quickly and gently. "Yes, you did. Don't move. Someone's at home in that house over there, and they'll call an ambulance."

Our racing friend returned from the house with a bag of ice.

I heard sirens and took a deep breath. Here I was, in my hot pink biking shorts, lying in the middle of the road. (I don't care how conditioned one's body is, bike shorts are too tight to be flattering, and I did not fall into the category of well-conditioned.) I closed my eyes, hoping to push the vision of the scene from my mind.

The sirens stopped. I looked up to see thirty or so men staring at me. I closed my eyes again and put my good arm over my face. I was the center of a flurry of motion.

A neck brace replaced my helmet. My arm was

scooped into a metal sling that looked like an open-ended French bread pan and stuck out at a weird angle. My shoulder stopped hurting. A female nurse from the ambulance took my pulse and blood pressure. She told me to breathe deeply to help slow my heart rate. I was put on a gurney.

All the while, those men, who were not figments of my imagination, watched. I peeked out from under my arm from time to time to see if they had left. They just stared.

As the attendants rolled me the short distance to the waiting vehicle, I thought, *I've gained too much weight. They'll never lift me up into the ambulance.* I kept my eyes closed.

"Stop!" the nurse yelled. "She won't go in."

Too heavy! I thought I would die from embarrassment.

"It's her arm. We'll have to load her at an angle." And they did.

We were off to the hospital. I got special treatment. I bypassed ER and went to a private room where I was prepared for surgery.

Surgery? For a broken arm?

The doctor told my husband, "This is extremely serious, even life-threatening. She has a compound fracture and the marrow of the bone has been exposed to air. We have to do surgery immediately."

My husband gave me a quick kiss as the gurney passed. "I love you."

"Me too." I whispered as the anesthesia took effect.

Surgery took six hours.

I got the best treatment ever during my hospital stay. The nurses checked my vitals every hour. Eight days later, I went home.

It was later I learned all the ways God's hand was in the events of that Saturday morning.

Regardless of where I had the accident, the ambulance would have had to come to the intersection where I lay. I was at the closest point of anywhere on the loop to the hospital.

Amazingly, someone was at home at that

intersection. The family that lived there usually had a stand at the farmer's market on Saturday mornings, but because of heavy rains the week before, they hadn't harvested their produce and didn't go to town. The next closest house was a mile away.

All those men who showed up had been in an EMT training session at the fire station about three miles from the intersection. They followed the ambulance for a live teaching session.

The doctor later told me how amazed he was that the nerve to my hand wasn't severed. The way the bones were broken, the nerve should have run over the jagged edge of the break. Normal movement on the ride to the hospital would have sliced the nerve. But because my hand was palm down (as my husband had placed it) instead of palm up (natural position) the nerve was frayed but not cut. The damage done should have limited use to my hand. But I eventually regained strength and coordination. The doctor was amazed.

I broke both bones in my forearm in two places.

With each break, the bones jammed through my skin and into the asphalt pavement. Grit, grime, and dirt was pulled inside my arm. All the special care I had received was because the bone was exposed to air. If I developed a fever, my arm would have to be amputated within an hour. No other options.

A renowned orthopedic surgeon was in the hospital that day. He was preparing for a difficult surgery on Monday and had come early to set up.

My shoulder was not broken, but the bones were bent forward and down about half an inch. Not noticeable, but I still cannot carry a purse strap on my left shoulder without it sliding off.

My recovery came in stages. I could use my arm after twenty weeks (five months), but I had no coordination or strength in my hand for almost two years. Even all these years later, I cannot hold anything in my arms for more than five minutes without it going limp.

My impact with the roadway was so hard I have an imprint of the pattern of the asphalt pressed into my helmet. The doctor said if I had not been wearing the helmet, the accident would have been fatal. As it was, I had a small abrasion (floor-burn) along my cheek.

The bike's handlebars were twisted but easily repaired. No other damage.

Since that Saturday morning, we've ridden around the neighborhood a few times, but I've never trained for another rally.

The Faith of a Child

When our son was two years old, he suffered from a rare form of epilepsy. At this age when his body should have been slowing down, he gained a half-inch in height each month. He was overactive, rarely rested, and got less than six hours of sleep a night. He began having seizures.

The doctors were baffled as to how to treat his condition. They had tested him with various treatments and drug combinations for months, and nothing seemed to work. They could control the seizures, but his growth rate increased. If they controlled the growth rate, he had more seizures.

Before giving up and establishing a maintenance plan, the doctors decided to try one last combination. A newly released drug would be used in addition to several other medicines. We hoped it would at least slow his growth rate and reduce the number of seizures.

The drug cocktail worked. However, I was concerned what the long-term effects from the heavy doses would have on a child so young. He stopped growing so fast and had no new seizures. At the age of three and a half, he was the size of a six-year-old. Six months later, he was on the growth charts for the first time in years. Albeit, at the top of the charts, but he was coming in range.

A well-known speaker came to a church about forty miles away. Since he was holding three services on Sunday, our pastor encouraged us to attend the two o'clock session.

It surprised us that close to fifty percent of the attendees at the afternoon meeting were from our church.

Only then did we learn it was a healing service. Oops.

I listened politely as the pastor made his impassioned plea for miracles. Most of what the man said whizzed over my head. Not because it wasn't relevant, but because I simply was not paying attention. Until right at the end of the service, when he said he would anoint anyone who wanted healing by putting a cross of oil on their foreheads, and Jesus would make them well.

I immediately thought of our son in the nursery.

My husband and I went to the play area.

"The preacher says he can put oil on your forehead, and Jesus will make you well. When he does that, you won't have to take your pills anymore." My husband's explanation was necessary because our son had seizures when he became frightened.

"Will it hurt?" Concern clouded his eyes.

"We don't think so. Do you want us to take you to the preacher man?"

The little one nodded.

His dad picked him up.

Together we took him down the side aisle to the altar and joined others who were already there.

The pastor put crosses on each forehead and prayed for each seeker as he moved down the row.

When he got to us, the pastor asked, "Why have you come?"

"I want Jesus to make me well." Our delightful child announced in a voice so loud everyone in the room heard.

He was anointed.

My husband returned our son to the nursery while I waited to hear the end of the sermon.

The pastor talked about results. The big question was, "When do you stop taking meds?" He suggested we continue medications until we see our doctor.

We drove the hour and a half home. For the first time since a newborn, our son fell asleep in the car.

That night when I fixed dinner, I put nine pills on his plate as usual. I'd make a doctor's appointment the next day.

When he came to the table, he looked at his plate and lifted it to me like a hungry child.

"Mommy, you forgot. I don't have to take my

pills anymore. Jesus made me well today."

"Oh, right." I gathered the pills with trembling hands. Had I put our son's life in danger. *Lord, please honor his faith.* I wanted to cry. Would he be okay?

I made the appointment. At our visit, the doctor reported his EEG was normal and we would begin to take him off his meds.

"But we must be careful." The man warned. "If he starts having seizures again bring him to the emergency room immediately. His seizures attack not only his brain but also his heart. So, don't delay, not even an hour. When he goes through puberty, we'll need to keep a close eye on him since kids with this condition frequently begin having grand mal seizures even with medication. Sometimes they are fatal."

I nodded. Fear gripped my heart.

I told him our son had not taken his meds for two weeks.

The doctor almost blew a gasket. "You have put

your child in great danger. He could have a grand mal seizure any minute, and it could kill him. You must continue his meds." He paused and stared at me. "I'm going to have you see my partner in the future. I don't deal with irresponsible parents."

What had I done? Was our son in grave danger because of my actions?

When we left the office, my son squeezed my hand. "He doesn't know Jesus can make people well, does he?"

"I don't think so." Fear, which had been growing, vanished.

I remembered the warning about grand mal seizures during puberty when our son turned twenty-one.

Surprise Reaction

I spent the afternoon at the outlet stores with a new friend. The lady began coming to our church in North Carolina about a month earlier. The second week she attended services, she received Christ as her Savior.

She was one fired-up new believer.

Since our kids were about the same ages, we bumped into each other in the hallway at church frequently, and it was time we got to know each other.

We had a fun day. We tried on dresses and shoes, checked out the latest jewelry, and learned to tie scarves six different ways. Between the two of us, we spent $10 – for lunch.

As I pulled into her driveway, we made plans to get together the next week.

"We've got an hour before the kids get home from school. Want to go get a Coke?" It seemed like the perfect way to end the day.

"No, not today. I need to do my horoscope."

"Oh." Her response surprised me. "You don't need to do that anymore. You have Christ now, and when we follow Him, He guides our steps. We trust Him, so we don't have to try to figure things out ourselves."

She had opened the car door but didn't get out. After a pause, she turned and looked at me. Confusion was written all over her face. She slid out of the car. "I'll see you Sunday." Then, she headed toward her house at a slow pace. Three times she turned and looked at me.

Such a strange reaction. I didn't leave until she walked through her front door.

When my husband got home from work, he informed me he had gotten a major promotion he had been seeking. And we would be moving to Michigan as soon as possible.

I chuckled about how the Lord guides our steps, many times in directions we least expect.

Sunday morning, my new friend pulled me aside before our Sunday School class.

"You really shook up my world Thursday." She almost bounced as she spoke.

"Really? How?"

"Remember you told me I didn't need to do my horoscope anymore?" I nodded.

"You didn't know this, but I studied horoscopes and constructed deeply involved charts. I had one whole room devoted to my practice of astrology. As I walked into my house, I knew you were right. I spent the whole afternoon getting rid of everything to do with horoscopes. I cried each step I took because I had grieved the Holy Spirit with my practice. It was as plain as day, and I'd never seen it before."

I could hardly breathe. I had no idea she was so wrapped up in that practice.

"I took out everything. Then I prayed in each

room asking for God's presence and protection."

While she spoke, her husband, a new believer also, joined us. He nodded. "As soon as I got home that night, I knew something major had changed. It was like the freshness that comes from pulling back the drapes and opening the windows. The darkness was gone."

"Wow! I didn't know."

Her husband grinned. "We filled four large trash bags with that stuff. Books, charts, wall hangings, jewelry, ephemeris, decorations. Everything."

My new friend gave me a quick hug. "Thank you for telling me the truth. You didn't judge. You simply stated a fact. I immediately understood what you said was true. Horoscopes are evil because they're against trusting God. Thanks to you, it's out of my life. A heavy burden has been lifted off my shoulders."

They turned and went to the New Believers class.

I stood in the empty hall. I didn't judge. Was it because I didn't know what was going on in her life?

Would my reaction have been different if I had known? I spoke God's truth. The simple statement was spontaneous. Words from God to her.

Because of a house-hunting trip to Michigan, our next get-together was cancelled. Two weeks later, we moved. My friend and I never talked in person again. We chatted on the phone several times. Her growth in faith and knowledge accelerated at rocket speed. We prayed for one another frequently.

After relocating I searched out classes on apologetics—learning to defend our faith. God had put his hand on that one visit but knowing techniques and expanding knowledge would be helpful in the future.

Our one-day shopping adventure changed both our lives dramatically.

Drive to Memphis

We live in Texas. Our son and his family live in Ohio, and we have relatives in Tennessee. When we visit, we drive and spend the night near Nashville.

One stretch of I-40 east of Memphis is exceptionally beautiful, especially in the morning with the sun at our backs. A gentle, well-mowed meadow separates east and westbound traffic by more than a quarter mile. The idyllic scene is peaceful, even with three lanes of traffic rushing to Memphis.

Several years ago, we arrived at this stretch of highway earlier than usual. A light mist in the lower section of the green valley glowed golden in the early morning sunlight. The beauty of that view made the drive through the large city at rush hour worth the trip.

Suddenly a car in the eastbound lane swerved into the meadow. I watched it descend the gentle slope to the bottom of the drainage area, dispelling the golden mist. The car didn't stop. It didn't even slow down. It started up our side of the median, barreling straight toward our lane of traffic.

"I can't move over. I can't slow down or speed up." My husband's voice was calm.

At the speed we were driving and the angle of the approaching missile, our paths would intersect in about twenty seconds.

"It's going to hit us, isn't it?"

There was no fear, just an acknowledgment of fact. The accident would be bad. The car would hit us, and we would careen into another lane. At least twelve cars would suffer significant damage and injuries. We would not survive.

My husband reached over and took my hand. "I love you."

"Me, too." I responded.

Life shifted into slow motion. We were trapped

in the inside lane. The car continued toward us. A peace I've never experienced surrounded me. No fear. No panic.

I prayed for the occupants of the other cars. I accepted my fate without arguing, but the others might need God's touch. I prayed for our family and asked God to be with them as they dealt with this incident.

Our estimate of the collision was accurate. The speeding blue mass would hit us just behind the front wheel.

As the car raced toward us, I fixated on the driver's side mirror. As it became more visible, I could clearly see three black streaks running from top to bottom. I focused on the insignificant to avoid the catastrophic.

I took my husband's hand in our last seconds before impact.

The inbound car bounced onto the shoulder of the road, caught the edge of the pavement, and jerked down the hill, missing us by inches.

We continued at 70 mph in silence.

Pure adrenaline ripped through me. The breath I had held exploded from my lungs, and I gasped to replace it. My heart thundered, and my eyes burned from staring without blinking. My insides churned. Disbelief mingled with joy, amazement, thankfulness, and terror.

After a few minutes, my husband squeezed my hand. “Thank you, Lord. By Your grace we were spared.”

Tears of joy flowed down my cheeks as I nodded, too grateful to speak.

That morning in west Tennessee, God protected us with His victorious right hand.

Rewards at the Beach

I don't like to fuss at kids, but I do want them to behave correctly. I reward good behavior while trying to ignore the not-so-good stuff. I learned this lesson one summer and have applied it frequently since.

I had taken my four grandchildren to the lake near our home. While they played in the water, I sat on the beach under my umbrella stabbed into the sand. I propped my feet up on the cooler.

We arrived mid-morning. I sat in the shade under the umbrella. The kids, three teenagers and one ten-year old, played in the water and on the beach. I read. The sun moved across the sky. Two hours later, I was in full sun.

It was time to go. The plan was to pack up, zip through McDonalds drive-thru, and go home for lunch.

"Time to go." I called to the kids. They waved in acknowledgement.

The ten-year old ran across the sand to help me gather our stuff. The other three headed to the floaters that marked the edge of the swim area – as far away as they could get.

My granddaughter and I must have been a sight trudging across the sand with the chairs, cooler, umbrella, and towels. As we approached the car, the three older kids showed up, grabbed towels, and hopped into the back seat.

They had disobeyed the call to leave. They hadn't helped. And they sat in the backseat giggling as the younger one and I lifted the stuff into the back of the car.

I was upset. We did all the work and were being mocked by three arrogant teens.

My prayer was short and to the point. "Lord, what do I do now? Give me wisdom."

The answer came immediately.

At McDonalds, I asked my helper what she wanted. Big Mac meal. I ordered two meals, three cheeseburgers and two orders of fries.

The giggling in the back seat stopped. No one said anything.

At home, my helper got her meal. I gave each of the others a sandwich and some fries. About halfway through lunch, one of the teens asked, "Why did she get a meal, and we only got a little burger and not even a whole order of fries?" Simple question.

"She helped me carry everything back to the car." Simple answer.

The next day, we went back to the beach. When the sun moved across the sky, it was time to go. I called to the kids, and they came running, all four of them. I barely got out of my chair before one of them folded it up.

I carried two towels back to the car.

At McDonalds, everyone ordered what he wanted. The bill was almost three times higher than the day before, but we were all happy.

And I hadn't fussed.

To this day, when I ask one of these three kids to do something, they do it immediately.

Life's Statement

My best friend in high school died recently. Our friendship spanned sixty years. She was maid-of-honor in my wedding. Although we were no longer best friends, we were good friends. We spent long weekends together twice a year.

My husband chuckled that she and I would see each other after months of separation and chat for hours and hours.

Over the last few years, I was aware that I talked about how God was working in my life. She listened politely but never responded. Instead, she discussed her charity work. Two years ago, I asked her if she knew Jesus as her personal Savior. She smiled and again told me how much time she spent helping others.

My heart was saddened. Some folks in my

generation feel uncomfortable talking about Jesus and God. I knew my friend had attended church as a teen, and she was still close to another friend who became a pastor.

My husband and I drove nine hours to attend her funeral. The morning of the service, the skies opened, and rain poured down in sheets. Streets were flooded and traffic rerouted. Such a gloomy occasion.

Our friend preached her eulogy. I waited for words of reassurance of her salvation. Instead, I heard tributes to her great deeds and accomplishments. He ended with, "she lived her life so we all would know her heart."

I almost cried. My friend was a good person who did good things. I don't know if she was a Christian. I'm hoping I will see her in heaven. Not because of her good deeds, but because at some point she acknowledged Christ as her Savior.

When I got home, I shared my concerns with my family. I pointed my finger at my granddaughters, then fourteen and seventeen, and said, “At my funeral, you have to stand up and proclaim that your grandmother loved Jesus as her personal savior.”

My shy, older granddaughter laughed. “I’ll never be able to do that. But don’t you worry, Grandma, everyone who knows you, knows you love God.”

That’s the way I want to live my life. So, everyone knows the things I do, I do for God. I’m a member of His family. He is my father and I love him.

The Tree of Life

After eighteen months of preparation, I was ready for our trip to Israel. The night before departure, I went over the list of supplies at least seven times. Odd little things like toilet paper, swim shoes, and trekking poles were carefully packed. One suitcase was only half full because I planned to collect many souvenirs along the way. Yes, I was ready.

When I sat to rest, my creative juices kicked in.

I'm a quilter and I love applique. What if, while touring, I found a design I could make into a wallhanging? I've never made my own applique pattern, but it couldn't be that hard, could it? Such a project would be really special.

And if everyone on our tour signed it, now, that would be cool! (I know, I know. That's a bit old fashioned, but it makes a point.) The best souvenir possible.

I rushed into my sewing room. I needed fabric, sandpaper so the fabric wouldn't slip when we wrote on it, and a fabric pen to get those signatures. I was still reorganizing following a minor flood and could only hope I put things where I could locate them.

"Lord," I prayed, "if you want me to make this happen, help me find the supplies."

Sometimes I think God sits on His throne and chuckles at us humans.

I immediately spotted the tan fabric that would be perfect. I trimmed off a fifteen-inch square. I opened the drawer where I keep pens, and right there were two, not one, but two, brown fabric pens. I tested them to be sure they were the right color with the tan fabric, and that they hadn't dried out. Perfect.

Now for the sandpaper. Where would I have put the sandpaper? I glanced at my sewing table still covered with odds and ends that needed to be put away. Right on top was an entire pack of super-fine grit paper. I was stunned.

I put the fabric, sandpaper, and pens into a large plastic bag, then into my suitcase.

The second night on the tour, I asked everyone to sign the fabric, and all forty-six folks did! I carefully folded the cloth and returned it to the bottom of the suitcase.

Throughout the trip, I took pictures of archeological sites, sewage drain covers, and motifs on walls. Then I saw it. At the top of a column among the ruins of the synagogue at Korazim was a design of six trees of life.

To Jews the tree of life is a symbol of Israel. To Christians, the simple pattern represents new life in Christ. Nothing could be more perfect. Remarkably, I took only one photo of the column.

Once home, I enlarged the picture so the image of one tree filled the space in my fifteen-inch square. I traced the design to make the applique template. It worked exactly as I envisioned.

I loved the sand-colored background I'd chosen. But the fabric for the tree was a different matter. At the fourth quilt store, I found it. A milk chocolate flannel with texture that caught the light at different angles and resembled stone.

I went to work. The project was made and quilted by hand. Using a machine or modern techniques seemed inappropriate to represent something thousands of years old.

As I stitched, I sensed the wallhanging should be gifted to our tour leader and his wife who are also friends. It would be a unique reminder to him of the special group of folks he led through the country where our Lord walked.

As the day approached for the presentation my anticipation grew. Would they like it? Would it mean as much to them as it did to me? Would they even understand what I'd done? What if…my stomach roiled. I wasn't even sure I wanted to give this special project away. But I told others what I planned, so I was committed.

I prepared two gifts. The husband received the picture of the column. The wife got the wallhanging.

When he opened the envelope, he recognized the column and briefly commented about its location. The tour guide was still at work.

I had rolled the wallhanging in tissue paper. The wife pulled what looked like a huge stuffed burrito from the fancy blue bag. “What is this?” She uncurled the mass. “Oh, my. Oh my.” She carefully lifted the wallhanging and held it for all to see. “Now this is really special.”

“It’s amazing.” Our guide’s voice broke. When he saw the signatures on the back, tears welled in his eyes. He nodded. No words needed.

After a few seconds, he took a deep breath. “It was a special trip. Thank you.”

Awakening

When we moved to northeast Pennsylvania, we located a beautiful old stone church in the denomination of our faith, the only one within fifty miles. The third Sunday we attended was the 100th anniversary of the church. The pastor had everyone who was related to one of the four founding families stand. All one hundred plus attendees stood except our family and one other.

The sermons were weak, the music stoic, but the people smiled. We believed this was where God wanted us. We would endure.

After six months however, we declared, to ourselves, this church was lukewarm, at best. We were tempted to say dead, but just because the fruits of the spirit weren't visible, that didn't mean He wasn't there.

We prayed.

I was asked to lead the children's church ministry. I have no idea why the group of ladies in charge decided I should take over this ministry. They must have been desperate.

The children's order of worship was simple and always the same. Greeting, two songs, Bible reading, prayer, offering, lesson, dismiss for snacks. For six months, the procedure was exactly the same regardless of how the students reacted. Even I was bored. I chafed at the lack of enthusiasm.

The songs were from the hymnal and one of the six melodies the unskilled piano player knew. Not exactly kid's songs. The Bible reading was from King James and the prayer a recited chant. The routine was so precise you could set your watch by the procedure.

I'm a teacher and understand children, especially how they learn. It was time for a change. When children get antsy, the service needed to be adjusted. This was an unknown concept to these people.

Yet, they agreed I could run the program as I saw best. If they had known what my techniques were, they'd have thought a little longer before they put me in charge.

The first Sunday I led children's church I taught the ten students a new song. The words were accompanied with hand motions and movement. The mystified piano player sat on the bench with her hands in her lap. The children sang enthusiastically. One of the helpers looked at her watch repeatedly. I was obviously running over on the allotted time for the song service.

The kids loved it.

By the end of the first month, I had taught my repertoire of piano-free songs. If the kids were restless, we sang more songs and cut the lecture time. One Sunday, I read the Bible verses first, before singing, and was confirmed a radical.

The amazing thing was kids were excited and inviting their friends to come. We grew to more than twenty kids over the next three months. The youngsters invited their parents, and the little cold church began to show signs of life.

The leaders climbed out of their rut. They opened to new ideas.

About this time, twelve couples began a study on prayer on Sunday nights. The first time we met, everyone wrote a prayer request only God could answer sometime within the next six months. We were not allowed to tell anyone what we wrote. We put the notes in envelopes with our names on them. When the prayer was answered, we were to take our envelope, open it, read the note to the group, and share what God had done.

The leader read the instructions without enthusiasm. I'm not sure he believed that God would answer. But he had learned to follow a published curriculum.

Most requests were simple. One man was so cynical, each time someone was excited because God had answered, he'd say, "Well, I can see how God did that. But he'll never answer mine. Just wait, you'll see.

Some things don't just happen."

One Sunday a young mother withdrew her envelope. As she held the sealed paper, tears started flowing. "I really didn't think God would answer this." Then she told her story.

For more than twenty years, her mother made a rainbow poke cake for her birthday. She wanted a chocolate fudge cake that her mother was famous for, but always got the traditional rainbow poke variety. She didn't like the special creation that took two days to make but wouldn't offend her mother by telling her. This year, when her mother arrived with the birthday cake, she apologized that she simply didn't have time to make the special rainbow cake and substituted a chocolate fudge cake.

The gal opened her envelope and held up the paper. "I want God to have my mother make a chocolate fudge cake for my birthday."

The group cheered. Even our cynic clapped. He leaned over, "That's great, but I'm afraid I put in a request that's impossible for even God to answer. I hope I don't ruin this little experiment for everyone."

Monday, we got a phone call from the church. A special service would be held Friday night. The Speer Family, a beloved singing group, would hold a concert.

The group's agent contacted our church when another engagement cancelled. They would come for a free-will offering and wave their normal booking fee. We were encouraged to invite friends.

The normally half-filled church was packed. I hadn't seen this congregation so excited about anything.

Sunday night our cynic stood. "I really didn't think God could do this. I really didn't" Tears flowed. He paused as he regained composure. "I knew our church couldn't afford them. I asked this because it was something I wanted." He opened his envelope. The paper read, "I pray that The Speers have a concert in our church." He added, "I didn't believe, but I do now. God is so much bigger than I knew. He can do anything." As he spoke, any remaining disbelief fell away like dead skin off a growing snake.

That lukewarm church erupted into a flaming beacon, led by the former cynic. Members welcomed the living God of the universe into their hearts. Their eagerness for God became impossible to stop. New Bible studies started. New members were welcomed. The meager choir filled out with beautiful voices. The new piano player in children's church wrote music for those *crazy* songs with motions. Excitement reigned. Their spiritual heartbeat strengthened.

A month later, we moved to Ohio. We picked up the envelope but never read our request, "We pray God will awaken this church and bring it to life." Amen.

Overcoming Fear

Driving on the interstate highways around Dallas +is frightening.

About forty years ago while living in Richardson, Texas, I had to enter LBJ Freeway on the right and and within a mile, cross six lanes of traffic to exit on the left in order to get to a meeting in Dallas. I did this every month for a year.

As I approached the entry ramp, my palms got sweaty, my stomach churned, and my entire body tensed. I faced lanes of whizzing cars and barreling trucks as I crossed the highway. I was terrified and prayed for safety. Each time I made it safely on my way, often to the blare of horns and unhappy, gesturing drivers.

Thankfully, no screeching brakes.

About six months into this adventure, my pastor

asked during his sermon, “What frightens you the most?”

I had an instant answer.

“Ask the Lord to help you. After all, we are not to live in fear but in victory with God.” (Jer. 10:8.) Sounded like an easy answer.

The next time I entered that treacherous ramp, I prayed. “Lord, help me negotiate this traffic. It scares me, and I don’t want to live in fear.”

When I pulled into the first lane, I glanced back to discover it was open--without any cars behind me for a quarter of a mile. As I moved across to the other side, each lane emptied as I needed to enter. When I exited, I praised the Lord for his help and proclaimed the victory He had given.

I don’t know what God did to those cars, but He cleared my path. He continued to clear lanes of traffic for me each time I entered the interstate.

To this day, every time I enter an interstate, I offer a quick prayer for help. Ninety percent of the time, the lane is clear at least eight or ten car lengths.

(But I still check before pulling into traffic.) I often tell passengers to look back and see what God has done.

Driving busy highways no longer frightens me, for I always travel with my Lord. I claim His victory every time I get behind the wheel. And I use these experiences to praise God for His constant presence.

Recently, I had another traffic problem. I got off the interstate on the left and within a quarter of a mile, I had to turn to the right. I arrived at this intersection during the height of rush hour, and all four lanes were filled with cars waiting for the light to change. Each time, I barely made it into the turn lane before the corner.

Again, my palms were sweaty and my body tense. I remembered my prayer for getting onto the interstate. “Lord, help me.”

I exited, but this time there were no cars on the entire access road. None. I easily crossed into the turn lane and went on my merry way, wondering what God did with all those cars that normally jammed the intersection. My joy could not be contained. I giggled at the miracle God performed. I sang praises.

I recalled the Johnny Appleseed song and changed the words to express my feelings.

The Lord is good to me, and so I praise the Lord.
For giving me the things I need,
His Son, His Spirit, and His book to read. The
Lord is good to me.

I have victory over my fears and the traffic on Dallas highways.

Nothing Just Happens

Nothing concerns moms as much as having a sick child. Both of my children had been sent home from school one day with fevers. I called the doctor and took both in for a check-up. We came home with four medications, two for each child.

Before bedtime, my ten-year-old's fever was gone. But the six-year-old was still sick. When I put them to bed, we prayed the medications would work, and they would be well by morning.

When dawn came, I awoke early and hurried to check on the six-year-old. He was hot and sweaty. My stomach lurched. I would need to explain how sometimes God says no to our prayers. I asked for wisdom.

An hour later, both children were up, playing, and hungry. No signs of any illnesses. Both fevers were gone.

When I told some ladies at church how God had honored our prayers, one replied, “When a child is hot and sweaty during the night, it means their fever broke.

It didn’t have anything to do with your prayers. It’s what happens when they take medicine.”

Another woman nodded. “Yes, it’s just circumstantial. Don’t go trying to give God credit for everything.”

I wanted to argue with them. *Don’t they see it was God who healed? He worked in my children’s lives.*

I simply said, “God is still in charge.”

How many times had I looked at circumstances and didn’t give God credit for His hand in the events? Little things like red lights when I needed to catch a breath, a rain shower when the garden needed watering and I had no time, or a calm spirit when being criticized. I just passed them off as circumstantial.

That morning in Bible study, I stopped believing in circumstances. That day, I became acutely aware that God is constantly at work in my life. I'm His child, and He's not going to toss incidents around haphazardly. Since that day, anytime things *just happen* I praise God for holding me in the palm of His hand.

He's here when things go as expected. He's also here when everything goes haywire. According to His promises, He will use everything to make me better and more Christ-like. (In my case, He still has a long way to go.) He plans each event as a learning experience to draw us closer to God and to trust Him more.

I'm not sure circumstances happen to any follower of Jesus Christ. I know they don't happen to me. All those *things that just happen* are spotlights from

God showing me He's still present and guiding me along my earthly journey.

And I *do* give God credit for everything.

The Nutcracker

For more than ten years, our family attended a performance of The Nutcracker at Christmas. The tradition began when a friend's daughter was in the ballet. After a few years we moved on to professional performances. The tradition became as important as gift giving.

When we traveled, we attend the ballet early in the season. If we stayed home, we'd go closer to Christmas. The time of the ballet dictated our holiday schedule.

One holiday, several years after my father passed away, my mother wanted all her children home for Christmas. She insisted everyone arrive for a family dinner a week before Christmas Day. She had a long list of activities for her three children and four grandchildren to accomplish during the week-long visit. Trips to the beach, Disney World, golfing, hiking, and seafood dinners at favorite restaurants.

Instead of building snowmen in Ohio, we would take dips in the pool in Florida. We exchanged our coats and mittens for shorts and T-shirts.

The day we left for Florida local performances of The Nutcracker opened in Ohio. Our plans were to attend the ballet presented by Disney Studios in Orlando. My mother thought that was a terrific idea and assured us we would attend. However, she did not reserve seats.

Soon after we arrived, I called to order tickets, only to learn all performances were sold out. I was so disappointed. This was our family's tradition. I called around to see if another group was presenting the ballet but didn't find one.

I had a choice. I could be sad our whole visit because a tradition was broken. Or I could rejoice in the birth of our Savior. Our family discussed other ways we could celebrate the holidays in a special way. Cookie making was out of the question. Too many people, too little space, and not my kitchen. The tree was already up, so tree trimming was out. As was gift wrapping.

Caroling wasn't even considered since we weren't good singers, and we didn't have the words. We thought of nothing and decided simply visiting Grandma in Florida would be special.

The adults visited on the porch and the children did crafts in the living room. My mother, a retired schoolteacher, had a different project each day. (No glitter.) My mom had a new golf cart which she let the kids drive around the neighborhood as long as an adult was present. Between golfing and trips to the pool, we relaxed. Time flew.

On December 22, my mom came out to the porch with her phone in her hand. "Anyone want to go see The Nutcracker tonight?"

"Yes." My husband, kids, and I chorused.

Mom's friend had gotten tickets for her family coming down from New York. They were already a day late arriving due to a snowstorm in North

Carolina. Because of unusually heavy traffic, they would not arrive in time to attend the performance. She had seven tickets which she gave to us.

My heart swelled with joy acknowledging that once again God provided. I saw the miracle he performed in giving us tickets. He knew our disappointment over missing the ballet and accomplished the impossible. My brothers didn't understand how extremely special this simple gift was. I was blessed beyond words.

Every Christmas, someone in our family comments on the Disney Nutcracker. Without a doubt that night was God's gift to my family.

The Gnarled Olive Tree

On the last day of our two-week tour of Israel, I found myself sitting on a cold stone bench with my back against the wall of the Church of All Nations. My tour group was walking down from the top of the Mount of Olives through the Jewish cemetery. Because of a knee problem, I was not allowed to descend the hundreds of steep steps and slick surfaces with them. Instead, I and two others were transported to the church via bus…and waited.

I stared at an ancient tree along the edge of an olive grove directly in front of me. The tree was not pretty with its rough bark, intertwined branches, and hollowed-out middle.

This was one of the sites in Israel that had a high probability of being a location where Jesus would have walked. Or in this case, prayed, on the night of

His betrayal. I was looking into the Garden of Gethsemane. Part of His final day was spent in this place.

My heart swelled with gratitude remembering all that Christ had done for mankind…and me.

A tour guide paused in front of me. With a quick hand gesture, he focused his followers' attention to the gnarled ugly tree.

"In all likelihood, this tree existed at the time of Christ." He continued with a scientific explanation of how to date a live tree since counting rings was impossible.

"All the trees in this orchard were dormant for at least four hundred years, possibly even a thousand. Yet, no one bothered to cut them down and plant a new orchard. In the summer of 1948, right after Israel became a nation again in May, every supposedly dead tree in the garden sent out new shoots. Every one of them. That summer, Israel and these trees resumed growing."

I gasped and goosebumps erupted along my

arms. How wonderfully God shows his power on earth. I stared at the gnarled tree and silently sang "Surely the Presence of the Lord Is in This Place."

How great is our God! He puts the world in place and controls the nations. He cares for every detail of our lives and is always with us. He causes dead trees to grow again.

How can I, a mere human, express my thankfulness to this great God? My soul sang praises to the Creator of the universe and to His Son who became a willing sacrifice so I could have a relationship with Him.

As I relaxed against that wall, the sounds of traffic faded. The masses of people visiting the site evaporated as I stared at the gnarled tree. I was aware only of the presence of God, and my heart sang even louder. A cloud of glory hugged me. The words of the hymn writers flashed through my mind. Even these were inadequate to praise Him.

My eyes filled with tears of worship.

My spirit soared.

I didn't move as I gazed at that tree. Love, adoration, and reverence flowed from within me. It would not have surprised me if the rapture occurred at that very moment.

After a period, I heard familiar voices. My group reached the church, and it was time to finish our tour. I didn't want to leave this place of peace beside the olive grove.

I had touched Heaven here.

I failed to take a picture of my gnarly tree, that at first glance looked more dead than alive. That's fine, because I could never have caught the image of my encounter. I left the garden with the scene engraved on my heart.

* * *

As a child of God, we are never alone. Nor does anything happen to us by chance. God is in control – of everything.

My prayer is that you walk closer to God today than yesterday. Remember the times God openly intervenes in your life and watch how those stories bless those around you.

Our lives are a great adventure.

Kathy Wall is a wife, mother of two, grandmother of eleven, and great-grandmother of twelve and counting. She's a retired fourth-grade teacher and was a foster parent for seven years. Her husband's job resulted in more than 40 moves. During that time, she began writing for local newspapers and branched into travel articles for regional and national magazines. She also began quilting.

After retiring, she began writing fiction and, to date, has published five romance novels. Quilting remains a passion. Many of her books include references to quilts and quilting techniques.

Today she and her husband reside near Dallas. They are active in their church and enjoy entertaining. In addition, she writes, quilts, and travels.

Books by Kathy Wall

Fiction:

The Gift Quilt

Trust Wyatt? No!

Never Again

Someone Special

The Lost Hero